Intercultural Communication and Body Language

JOHANNES GALLI

Toronto Oct 17 '01

You can view the complete program
of the Galli Publishing House
on the Internet at:

http://www.galli.de

or

http://www.galli-group.com

1. edition 2000
All rights reserved.
ISBN: 1-58619-023-7
Library of Congress Card Catalogue No. 00-111440

Translation:
Caroline Hayes, Dale Whinnett

Cover photographs:
Galli Archives and Georg Nemec

Cover and text design:
Sarah Watson Design

Printed in Canada
January 2001

ELTON-WOLF PUBLISHING

2505 Second Avenue Suite 515   Seattle, Washington 98121
Tel 206.748.0345 Fax 206.748.0343
www.elton-wolf.com info@elton-wolf.com
Seattle • Los Angeles

Contents

The Galli Business Theater team in a motivational theater production called *The Secret of Success* for the DaimlerChrysler Corporation.

PHOTOGRAPH BY RAINER SCHMIDT

Preface

Galli is an internationally active enterprise and, like all of its licensed single businesses, carries the name of its founder, Johannes Galli.

In the last fifteen years, the business theater presentations and intercultural training courses have made the name GALLI into an international quality standard for creative and effective communication. With its repertoire of more than seventy motivational theater pieces, the Galli Business Theater employs its services over 150 times annually with internationally renowned companies such as the Allianz Group, DaimlerChrysler, The Dow Chemical Company, BP Oil, BMW, Audi, Arthur D. Little International, BASF, Hewlett Packard, and Siemens. The Galli Business Theater is known for its innovation, poignancy, flexibility, and inspiration.

In the Galli training courses, instruction is given for overcoming old structures, experiencing new frontiers, and activating unimagined resources of creativity. The courses aim to teach flexibility, high motivation, clear vision, persuasive body language, dynamic speech, optimal presentation, and effective communication.

It has been proven again and again that the core of the Galli Method, which encompasses spontaneous role-play, presents an excellent opportunity to experience communicative situations in daily business life from a creative new point of view.

A scene from the Galli Business Theater piece
Lady Client and King Arthur talking about
customer orientation.

PHOTOGRAPH BY GEORG NEMEC

Intercultural Communication and Body Language

Participants in a Galli Training *Effective Communication* working on their personal expressiveness.

Introduction

Anyone who thinks about misunderstandings caused by body language immediately recalls experiences in foreign countries where they understood the language only slightly or not at all. Whether such misunderstandings result in laughter or embarrassingly tense silences depends upon how quickly and openheartedly the misunderstandings can be explained on both sides.

The following examples are intended to create an awareness of body language in its simplest form and to show the types of unpleasant misunderstandings that can arise unexpectedly:

- The thumbs-up sign is interpreted as a positive signal in the sense of "Everything is all right", but also is the typical sign used by hitchhikers to show that they need a ride. These are the common meanings in North America and Europe, whereas in Asia and Africa, if the thumb is stuck up and moved in an upward motion it becomes a phallic symbol and is interpreted as a rude, sexual affront.

- The "okay" sign is a circle formed by the index finger and the thumb and is understood differently in various parts of the world. For scuba divers who cannot verbally communicate underwater, this sign means "Everything is okay". In Greece, Turkey or Russia, however, this gesture symbolizes a human posterior opening in the lower body and is considered highly obscene.

- One can experience a great deal of confusion when visiting an Indian market. Shaking the head means "yes" there, while a European perceives this gesture as a clear "no". These two opposite meanings for the same gesture can cause serious misunderstandings.

The differences in these cultural examples are wonderfully suited for creating awareness of the fact that a basic knowledge of body language is very useful. In business and in private life, its absence can result in miscommunication that not only hinders reaching your objective, but it can even achieve the opposite of what was intended.

Small misunderstandings that arise through communication made with body language can be economically costly.

My main concerns are the small misunderstandings that arise through communication made with body language, which can be economically costly. Just as in a poker game when a slight twitch of the eye betrays what is hidden, body language, both in business or in one's personal life, can expose an attempted lie or confirm one. One could even maintain that the most important information is sent and received via body language while verbal expressions convey less significance.

Intercultural Communication and Body Language is a report based on experience with different intercultural projects on which I worked in 1998. I received support from various international firms who, in the era of globalization, had shown an enormous need for training courses in this ever-growing field. Because of global interaction, contact between foreign cultures and business cultures results in communicative misunderstandings, which obviously become extremely expensive for business organizations.

Through training courses, lectures, and individual consultations, I helped detect misunderstandings caused by culturally differing strategies and then, using the Galli Method, I employed acting skills to resolve them. This was a highly enjoyable task for me as it permitted me to teach and do research at the same time.

I thoroughly examined the sources of misunderstandings and mistakes associated with intercultural communication. Surprisingly, language barriers had not caused the majority of these. It was not caused by ignorance but was due to a lack of awareness regarding how we communicate via our body movements. Once I understood the source of the confusion, it was my task to create an awareness of body language!

Johannes Galli in an intercultural training for sales managers of BP Oil.

PHOTOGRAPH BY GALLI ARCHIVES

The Need for Intercultural Communication

More and more businesses and economic, political, and cultural institutions, now networked worldwide, find themselves forced to devote more time and energy to intercultural processes than they had originally planned. Many had thought that as soon as they were networked, everything else would follow automatically. They were wrong. Prejudices held against foreign cultures don't automatically disappear nor do they vanish over a period of time. On the contrary, many business people find themselves confirming their prejudices, thereby widening the divisions. Learning a foreign language is beneficial but, if the prevention of misunderstandings is not conscientiously worked on by becoming aware of body language, there will always be a danger that misunderstandings will continue. This will result in negative and expensive consequences.

If the prevention of misunderstandings is not conscientiously worked on by becoming aware of body language, there will always be a danger that misunderstandings will continue.

During my German philosophy and history studies, I not only garnered financial stability by teaching German courses to foreigners, but also used this unique opportunity to delve into the foreign cultures I encountered. I realized the necessity of teaching the basic knowledge of body language to my students, who were earnestly interested in learning about German culture. This was especially true of the young men who naturally wanted to understand the body language of German "fräuleins". Exchanges between the sexes illustrated the importance of foreigners understanding body language. Teaching my students how to read fräulein body language helped break the endless chain of misunderstandings they encountered in a foreign country.

Between 1979 and 1982, I worked throughout Europe for the Goethe Institute. It became increasingly apparent to me that to meet the needs of the students from virtually all over the world, it was necessary to direct one's consciousness toward one's own body language and that of the person being encountered.

I vividly remember a conversation I had during a break with a young Chinese woman who complained to me that a young Persian had come so close to her that she had felt insulted. When I spoke to the young Persian during the next break, I began to understand the problem. He stood very close to me throughout the entire conversation and placed his hand on my lower arm, patted me on the shoulder and ignored my efforts to keep a healthy distance according to European standards (about an arm's length).

In a long talk that followed, I asked the young Chinese woman and the Persian man to reenact the situation and show what had happened when the conflict arose. By speaking with them and studying their interaction, I was able to resolve the friction between the two. This reaffirmed my belief that body language is a critical and underestimated factor in the process of communication between two cultures.

Dr. Nieder, the former Director of the Freiburger Goethe Institute, supported my insistence on giving greater consideration to body language in language courses. He made it possible for me to use a semester researching my find. Dr. Nieder was coauthor of the Goethe Institute's standard work: *Braun-Nieder-Schmöe: Deutsch für Ausländer* (German for Foreigners). I owe him my profound gratitude. Through his encouragement and support, I was permitted to freely research the characteristics of body language in different cultures.

Body language is a critical and underestimated factor in the process of communication between two cultures.

I asked my students to act out small theatrical scenes in German dealing with daily life such as "Shopping", or "The Flirt", or "A Conversation with a Policeman", or "What is typically German?"

In the scene "What is typically German?" students from different cultures acted out what their strongest impressions of Germany were since they arrived. I was amazed by the precision with which people from faraway countries could spontaneously portray the German character, having spent so little time in Germany.

As my life's path led me away from the academic arena so that I could further develop my skills in the theater, my research work on intercultural body language was temporarily discontinued. Later, when my theater work and my training method became important to international companies, I, once again, found the time, space, motivation, and inspiration to take up the study of intercultural body language and communication.

The participants in my body language courses in Europe listened more closely the more foreign the culture I described.

One thing in particular had caught my attention. The participants in my body language courses in Europe listened more closely the more foreign the culture I described. If I told them about my experiences in the People's Republic of China, they listened carefully to every word. If, however, I was explaining the need for awareness of body language in their workplace, I had to struggle to prove that it was a significant topic for them in their daily interactions. Although foreign descriptions create attentiveness, it was then, and still is, important to me to direct awareness toward our body language in daily life. (See also the Galli books *Body Language and Communication* and *Effective Communication*, Galli Publishing.)

In my training courses, the stories of confrontations with foreign cultures create an exciting beginning for the necessary discussion on body language awareness. This is especially true in business.

Current globalization has opened the gateway to extensive research and teaching projects that deal with the blending of different cultures through body language. In the following overview, I relate interesting aspects of human life that a person in a foreign culture might encounter. I use a series of questions to provide a map of ideas. In accordance with the Galli Method, I don't offer answers to these questions; rather they form the foundation of various scenes in which the players portray culturally characterized differences. They resolve these differences in the performances.

In an initial overview, I present seven situations in a foreign culture that can be experienced through acting out:

1. Family Life

2. Business Life

3. The Network of Relationships

4. Eating Rituals

5. Love Life—Flirting and Marriage

6. Relationship to Money

7. Religion and Spirituality (misunderstandings and resolving conflicts)

Through a variety of questions, I direct participants' awareness to areas where there may be a need for familiarity with foreign rules of communication and body language. By doing this, they are brought closer to a better understanding of those with whom they're in contact and they're shown conflict resolution skills.

At the beginning of the series of questions, I introduce an idea for a skit. As the word 'skit' suggests, it is an idea, a suggestion, a possibility, or a starting point. Every firm, every institution, and every society that is working on intercultural communication and body language will have its own unique ideas about the topics they want to emphasize. The suggestions I provide for the skit and the associated questions are not meant to inhibit the imagination, but to stimulate it.

As the word 'skit' suggests, it is an idea, a suggestion, a possibility, or a starting point.

The courage to transform even the most difficult situation into the scene of a play defines the usefulness and the power of the method. The method enables the individual's imagination to explore new realms of effective communication.

Perfect Service — a Galli Feedback Theater skit. Feedback theater encourages the participants of a training to experience new skills they developed in the training. While playing, they give feedback to the actual process. In this case, it was a quality improvement training for the Dow Chemical Company.

PHOTOGRAPH BY GALLI ARCHIVES

1. Family Life

Idea for a skit: "The family get-together"

A typical family get-together is held and you, as a foreigner, are invited. The foreigner enters the family group as a guest. The guest has many questions, such as:

◎ *How do I dress?*

◎ *How do I address the host?*

◎ *Is it appropriate to bring a gift?*

◎ *How do I act toward the different members of the family?*

◎ *What will be the topic of conversation—personal, business, or social?*

People appreciate this skit because the likelihood of being a guest in a foreign home is common and the skit presents a good opportunity for practicing an actual event.

The likelihood of being a guest in a foreign home is common and the skit presents a good opportunity for practicing an actual event.

2. Business Life

Idea for a skit: "New on the team"

You are new to the company. The boss introduces you to the team you'll be working with. A team acquires a new worker. The new teammate explores the following questions:

◎ *How will the others on your team handle this change?*

◎ *What do you initially talk about—personal subjects or business?*

◎ *Do the individuals at the company embrace the team concept or is there a more hierarchical way of thinking?*

◎ *Are there any unwritten rules in the workplace that you should know?*

◎ *How is initiative appreciated?*

◎ *How are innovative ideas grasped and encouraged?*

3. The Network of Relationships

Idea for a skit: "Your friend helped you"

Your friend has selflessly helped you in a difficult situation. How do you show your gratitude? With money? An invitation? A gift? Your friend helped you in a difficult situation and now you must decide how to respond.

◉ *How do you thank the person for the help? With an invitation to dinner? With an invitation for a drink? With a gift? With money?*

◉ *What does the acquaintance, the relative, or the friend expect in return for the service he or she has offered?*

◉ *When and on what occasions can you address another person informally? What ritual is used to introduce this new level of the relationship?*

There are several scenarios in this skit that make it fun to act out and the results are immensely rewarding.

4. Eating rituals

Idea for a skit: "Invitation to dinner"

Your friend helped you in a difficult situation and now you must decide how to respond.

Everything is acted out, from the invitation to dinner, to the giving of the gift, to the end of the meal and the clearing of the table. One or more people are invited to dinner by one or more hosts. The occasion for the invitation can be of a friendly, personal, or business nature. It can also be a birthday dinner or other occasion for celebration. Many factors need to be considered in this situation by both the host and the guest:

◉ *When do you invite someone to dinner? Is there a dress code?*

◉ *What kinds of gifts are expected?*

◉ *Who is responsible for the dinner menu? How many courses are included in a typical meal for the country? What are the typical appetizers, main courses, and desserts?*

◎ *What role does meat with meals play? Is there a vegetarian tradition?*

◎ *What role does smoking play during the meal?*

◎ *What do you drink with the meal? What role does alcohol play?*

◎ *Typically, how long does a meal with friends last?*

◎ *Which rituals accompany the meal? Is a prayer said or a speech given?*

◎ *What defines a business meal?*

◎ *What is a typical ritual that ends the meal?*

5. Love Life—Flirting and Marriage

Idea for a skit: "Evening in the park"

You went to the movies together and then out to eat. Now the two of you are sitting on a park bench in the light of the full moon on a beautiful spring night. In this skit, the focus is on practicing the delicate steps of approach between a man and a woman. The following questions are to be considered in this skit:

The focus is on practicing the delicate steps of approach between a man and a woman.

◎ *Who plays the active role in the advances between a man and a woman?*

◎ *Are there clear taboos between men and women?*

◎ *What words and actions are inappropriate and insulting to the woman's dignity? To the man's?*

◎ *How is sexuality defined? Is it recreation-oriented or is it taken more seriously?*

◎ *What role does the engagement play? What rituals are usual for weddings? How is the institution of marriage socially anchored?*

6. Relationship to Money

Idea for a skit: "Bargaining at the market"

You're with your new friend or associate. You want to buy something at the market. You begin to bargain and try to figure out how far below the set price the seller will go. After bartering and buying, you go to a bar, a café, or a restaurant and discuss money.

◎ *How openly are the profits, turnover, and salaries of a firm discussed?*

◎ *What is especially expensive and especially cheap in this country?*

◎ *Do you give tips? How much is expected? Do you overtip the expected amount? Do you leave the money lying on the table or hand it to the waiter?*

7. Religion and Spirituality

Idea for a skit: "Going to Mass together"

How do you act with respect for the religious beliefs of others?

You are invited to go to Mass or a religious service. How do you act with respect for the religious beliefs of others? The following questions are asked and discussed:

◎ *What are the primary religious values and institutions of the country you are visiting? Which religion dominates?*

◎ *Are "foreign" religions integrated in this society?*

◎ *What is the connection between business and religion?*

◎ *What is the central message of the founder of the predominate religion?*

Since religion is a highly personal subject, a great deal of tact is required for acting out this skit.

These seven examples are the touchstone from which other effective skits may be developed. They can be playacted according to the needs of the individuals. They enable a visitor to a country to become familiar in dealing with a foreign culture.

It must be mentioned that intercultural communication is not only important between two cultures but also within the same culture. A person within the same culture moves from the countryside to the city and is confronted with unfamiliar forms of conduct which he or she experiences but doesn't immediately understand.

A big shift of priorities is taking place in the business world. The emergence of globalization has resulted in more and more firms, previous competitors, consolidating in order to remain competitive in the world market. The consolidation of two unique firms inevitably results in the clashing of two different company cultures.

Intercultural communication is not only important between two cultures but also within the same culture.

In the last few years of my training courses, I have often had the task of guiding the difficult process of helping merge two business cultures into one.

On August 12, 1998, I gave a speech at the premiere of my intercultural theater piece *Conciliation Part II* at the Royal Saskatchewan Museum in Regina, the capital of the Canadian province of Saskatchewan.

This piece, played by German actors and Canadian Native Indians, was aimed at deepening the understanding between the Indian and European-Canadian cultures. The goal of *Conciliation Part II* was to stimulate the process of reconciliation between Canadian culture and the Native Indians, which had begun to falter and deteriorate.

This is the goal—to achieve understanding by understanding communication.

"*Only by understanding the cultural achievements of other people will we be able to also develop understanding for one another. If we do not succeed in this, then we will perceive everything foreign as threatening and believe that we need to aggressively protect ourselves. Intercultural exchange is the core of my vision, which is to create the foundations for enabling people to understand themselves and others better.*

"*This is the goal—to achieve understanding by understanding communication. This is the goal that should not only be strived for by individuals in daily contact with other individuals, but by all cultures which need to be brought closer together in order to live peacefully in this world.*"

The Galli Method®

The Galli Method resurrects worn-out processes, breaks through hardened structures, dissolves them, and presents surprising alternatives for seemingly unsolvable conflicts. In short, the Galli Method brings them to life.

How does it do this?

Most of the people in the world use intellectual strategies for communication. This is illustrated by the importance assigned to electronic communication. Through this process, the significance of body language and the language of emotions is greatly underestimated. A brief look at the political, economic, social, and cultural situations in the world shows that a predominantly intellectually oriented approach can quickly lead to the conventional stifling of all growth processes. The need for a method that enlivens and perpetuates creative growth is clear.

The Galli Method begins at the point when intellectual strategies have ceased to work and when processes have long become stagnant. It endeavors to transform courses of action, familiar to almost every institution, into a flowing, lifelike process.

The key word in the Galli Method is **"acting"**. The Galli Method maintains that when the participants use a theatrical scene to act out problems, conflicts, or processes, a solution becomes possible. This theory must be explained to the skeptical person while the practical-minded will learn by doing it.

Out of habit, the skeptic initially likes to understand the Galli Method intellectually. But the acting forces the individual to participate in *creatively* reaching a solution.

To act out a process means to copy it so that it can be reproduced. This requires an act of consciousness. The player must recall a course of action that takes place in daily life automatically, and then he or she portrays it. The players have to exchange their internal experience for external experience. Once they observe themselves

A predominately intellectually oriented approach can quickly lead to the conventional stifling of all growth processes.

from the outside, they are then capable of achieving extraordinary results. Not only do they break out of their habitual behavior, but they also confront this behavior by interpreting it through their acting.

Because the players are able to observe themselves from the outside, they can be more successful in portraying a situation. And, by confronting himself with his external appearance, the actor is better able to penetrate his inner world of experience.

Within the complete freedom of the play and the pleasant relaxation it brings, a solution appears that the daily pressure to achieve may have suppressed.

The individual plays himself. Within the complete freedom of the play and the pleasant relaxation it brings, a solution appears that the daily pressure to achieve may have suppressed. Taking scenes from the actor's private life enhances the experience. The conflict that has just been acted out is placed in a new framework.

The practical aspect of this process is that the Galli Method is uncomplicated to implement. As the old saying goes, "To be effective it has to be simple" or, as the Americans would say, "Keep it simple!" The Galli Method is so easy that you don't need anything other than trust and courage. You don't need a theater or spotlights or videos or flip charts or overhead projectors or folders or gadgets or halls, not even a conference room.

The courage and trust of the participants, a competent trainer, and a few minor supplies are all that are required. A room must be set up and designated as the "stage". The people who enter it are referred to as the "actors". Seating is provided and those who occupy it are referred to as "the audience". A trainer is required but only assumes the role of moderator and is referred to accordingly. All that remains to be said is, "Let the show begin!"

Galli Business Theater as part of a sales training. The Siemens sales and marketing managers were trained to pay attention to the *Seven Rules for Effective Communication.*

PHOTOGRAPH BY GALLI ARCHIVES

The Seven Rules
for Effective Communication

Participants in the *Body Language and Communication* courses almost always want rules. They want something in black and white that they can take home with them. The rules that I offered are not rules in the usual sense, but mere suggestions that they should take note of. It would be correct to define them as "The Seven Hints for Paying Close Attention to Body Language". They all begin with the words "Pay attention to ..." and explain only what one should notice —the need for opening one's powers of perception.

From early childhood, we're used to physically expressing nearly all impressions and expressions using body language.

Body language is not something foreign that we have to learn. It belongs to us—just like our bodies! From early childhood we're used to physically expressing nearly all impressions and expressions using body language. During puberty, we experience an alienation from our bodies because we're exposed to a very strong value-judgment system. It tells us what is beautiful and what is ugly, creating an ideal that we can never achieve. Body language is not something that you have to learn for the first time. You simply have to remember how you

Intercultural meeting at the Mercedes Benz museum: The Galli Business Theater actors with the IOC President Mr. Samaranch.

PHOTOGRAPH BY DAIMLERCHRYSLER

used to communicate before restrictions were placed on the way you used your body.

The *Seven Rules for Effective Communication* arose from the need to provide the methodology for communicating in diverse situations. An introduction to the skills is necessary if you don't want to be swept away by your unconscious prejudices, misunderstandings, and unresolved feelings. These factors influence communication a lot more than we would like to admit, even to ourselves.

We benefit by considering the following gestures:

- posture
- movements
- voice
- timing
- glances
- language
- breathing
- appropriateness

These help us recognize concealed information about a situation and our personal world much faster, more clearly, and more subtly. We can save ourselves time by focusing on what's happening quickly and precisely. As a result, we can make the most of it.

The *Seven Rules* were created to look behind the scenes in daily private and professional life in order to receive more profound information about ourselves and others.

At a time when the saying "time is money" is particularly true, the ability to make quick and accurate decisions is worth its weight in gold. Today, with the economy in the throes of a process of transformation, the ability of employees to communicate is a key factor in a corporation's success.

Today, with the economy in the throes of a process of transformation, the ability of employees to communicate is a key factor in a corporation's success.

The *Seven Rules,* which are shown on the following pages, are made up of a series of questions that serve to guide the observer. They enable him to take a wide range of factors into consideration when appraising a situation. After each rule are exercises which make it easy for the reader to structure his daily observations.

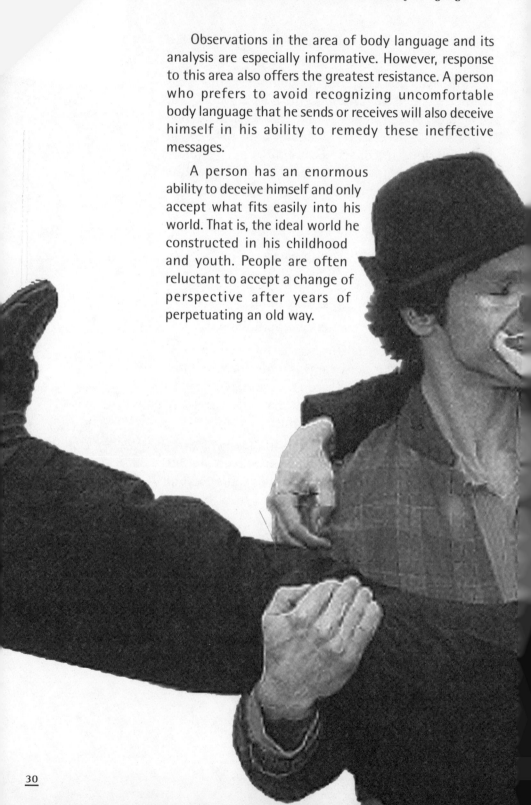

Observations in the area of body language and its analysis are especially informative. However, response to this area also offers the greatest resistance. A person who prefers to avoid recognizing uncomfortable body language that he sends or receives will also deceive himself in his ability to remedy these ineffective messages.

A person has an enormous ability to deceive himself and only accept what fits easily into his world. That is, the ideal world he constructed in his childhood and youth. People are often reluctant to accept a change of perspective after years of perpetuating an old way.

Intercultural Communication and Body Language

This is not intended as a general complaint about the unwillingness of people to get to know and understand themselves but as a serious reminder to be aware of this unfortunate basic attitude. This is especially true with regard to body language. Most people intuitively understand the body language of other people but are reluctant to accept it because this under- standing does not reflect their own character in the most admirable light.

The *Fun of Failing* is the title of Johannes Galli's most famous book in which he describes the essence of the clown. It was also the title of a Galli Business Theater piece for the Audi Volkswagen Company.

PHOTOGRAPH BY AXL JANSEN FOR LUFTHANSA MAGAZINE

To really understand body language is to accept the unacceptable in one's own character. Only then does body language become an effective tool for learning about yourself, bearing in mind that your own body language also influences the body language of others.

Observing body language is not about learning something new but about activating the old knowledge, which resides in each of us.

Observing body language is not about learning something new but about activating the old knowledge, which resides in each of us. It needs only to be recognized and appreciated with a new awareness.

The Seven Rules for Effective Communication:

1. *Pay attention to posture and the distance between people.*

2. *Pay attention to movements.*

3. *Pay attention to the look.*

4. *Pay attention to language. Are the words full of imagery and is the tone in a steady voice?*

5. *Pay attention to breathing.*

6. *Pay attention to the timing.*

7. *Pay attention to the appropriateness of the situation.*

Here's a suggestion for trainers in workshops and courses on body language and communication:

Questioning the individual's rules of behavior forms the basis for interpreting a skit. These questions, although they only represent a small segment of the whole, can reveal unexpected depth in your own character as well.

The following exercises are a way to intensify the ability to study your own body language, as well as that of others.

Rule One

*Pay attention to posture and
the distance between people.*

Posture and the distance between people form the foundation for the series of observations we will use to heighten our awareness in particular situations.

At the beginning of an encounter, the following questions focus our attention on the basic posture of the bodies. (Keep in mind that you should apply these questions to yourself.)

◎ *Is the other person standing erect or is she slouching? Do I find her physically pleasant or is she too fat, too thin?*

◎ *Is she standing upright or is she leaning on something?*

◎ *Is her pelvis tilted, are her feet next to one another or is she taking a step?*

◎ *Are her arms folded across her chest or hanging loose?*

◎ *Are her hands holding onto something tightly, are they in her pants pockets, or hanging at ease at her sides?*

◎ *Is she stretching her head upward, is her head hanging or tilted to the side?*

◎ *Is the distance between the other person and me comfortable for me?*

◎ *Did I take into account that the polite distance for communication in America is an arm's length and that other cultures find other distances ideal?*

◎ *Is the other person standing too close or do I need to take a step back to create the "right" space between our bodies?*

◎ *Is the other person too far away or do I feel the need to come closer to create the "right" space between our bodies?*

*Posture and the
distance between
people form the
foundation for the
series of observations
we will use to
heighten our
awareness in
particular situations.*

Exercises

1. How is my posture?

Describe your body in terms of the questions on the previous page. Stand in front of a large mirror and carefully study your image before you start to write.

2. What sensations and feelings do I have when I observe my body?

Describe the sensations and feelings you experience when you look at yourself without improving on or judging your image in the mirror. (Remember that striving for the ideal figure enormously hinders objective observation.)

3. Do I pay attention to the distance between people?

Describe whether you are more of the "friendly" type who likes standing close to people and touching them or are you more of the "shy" type who would rather stand at a secure distance and avoid touching?

Rule Two

Pay attention to movements.

It's surprising how much information one gets about others when paying attention to how they move.

It's surprising how much information one gets about others when paying attention to how they move. It's not only the way they walk that tells us about their inner thoughts and feelings, but also the way they sit, stand, turn, and greet others. It becomes obvious that every person has a different basic speed at which he or she carries out movements. Often a revelation occurs when dancing with another; when you experience his feeling for rhythm or the dynamics of her movement.

The following questions give a glimpse into the vast field of human forms of movement:

◎ *How does the other person move? Controlled or restlessly?*

◎ *How does he walk? Brashly or sluggishly? Like he's skipping or like he's carrying a heavy load?*

◎ *Are her movements steady and thoughtful or twitching and abrupt?*

◎ *What is his basic form of movement—a little too slow or too fast?*

◎ *Does she make other movements that she's not aware of, like running her fingers through her hair, twitching her leg, drumming her fingers on the table?*

◎ *Describe the pressure of his handshake. Is it limp or firm and energetic?*

◎ *How does the other person dance, with a confident rhythm or insecurely and offbeat?*

Ask your friends how they view your movements.

Exercises

1. How do I move?

Describe how you analyzed your own movements with the help of the "Pay attention to movements" questions.

2. How do others view my movements?

Ask your friends how they view your movements. Write down their perceptions, including direct quotations. Be sure to encourage them to share physical details.

3. How do I dance?

Dance before a large mirror. Describe how you dance. Are there forms of movement that you shy away from because it might move something inside you that you don't want moved?

Rule Three

Pay attention to the look.

The eye is the *window to the soul* and everyone knows how enormously important it is. It's how we look at others and how others look at us. In one glance, ideas are transmitted. We should be careful at whom we look and why. There's a reason many cultures don't allow the women to look directly at a man but require they look to the ground. If a man looks into a woman's eyes with desire or attraction, he is considered to have penetrated very deep inside her.

Studying the eye, the *window to the soul*, is one way we can become more aware of our distinctive cultural differences. Ask the following questions:

Studying the eye, the window to the soul, is one way we can become more aware of our distinctive cultural differences.

◎ *Does the other person have an open look or a guarded one?*

◎ *Does he look long into my eyes or does he look away immediately after looking into my eyes?*

◎ *When he speaks to me, does he look at me or does he look beyond me, above me, or below me?*

◎ *Is his glance intense or more guarded?*

◎ *Do I have the feeling that he is really looking at me, trying to understand me, or is his glance shallow and purely businesslike?*

◎ *Is his glance electric and radiating (projecting outward) or magnetic (drawing the object of his gaze, in)?*

Exercises

1. *Looking in the mirror, I look myself straight in the eyes.*

Describe your gaze. For suggested observations, use the questions from Rule Three: "Pay attention to the look."

2. *I ask friends about my gaze.*

Write down exactly what they say when you ask your friends to describe your gaze.

3. *I observe and change my look.*

Describe your feelings when you change your look by imagining different situations. What connections do you see between your thoughts and the expressions on your face?

Rule Four

Pay attention to language. Are the words full of imagery and is the tone in a steady voice?

Everyone is familiar with the startling experience of a voice that doesn't fit the person it belongs to. How often have we formed a distinct impression of how a person looks after the first telephone conversation and when we meet them, we're surprised because their physical appearance didn't fit their voice at all? This familiar experience shows how strongly a voice influences and stimulates our imagination. It's not just the voice itself, but also the choice of words that prompts our associations.

A simple rule about word choice—the more you use imagery while speaking, the more you reach the other person's heart. The more abstractly we speak, the more we reach the intellect.

The more you use imagery while speaking, the more you reach the other person's heart.

As we turn our attention to speech and voice, keep these questions in mind:

◉ *How does the other person speak, too quickly or too slowly?*

◉ *Does she use imagery, examples and comparisons?*

◉ *Does she speak with her whole body, using expressions and gestures to reinforce what she is saying or does her body barely support her statements? How does her voice sound, too high or too low?*

◉ *Is she easy to understand or does she speak unclearly, mumbling, lisping or even stuttering?*

◉ *Does the volume of her voice fit the situation or is it always the same? Always monotone or always excited?*

◉ *Does her voice seem free and direct or do you have the feeling that she holds it in her throat, refrains, or suppresses her desire to speak freely?*

Exercises

1. What is my language like?

Considering the questions from Rule Four, "Pay attention to language", describe whether you use language filled with imagery or language that is more abstract, too general and lacking details? Are you content with your style of language or would you like to improve it? If so, in what way?

2. Do I speak foreign languages?

Count the number of foreign languages you speak and describe how your feelings change when you change from speaking one foreign language to speaking another foreign language or speaking your normal, everyday language.

3. How does my voice sound?

Consciously listen to your voice or record it on tape and then listen to it. Write down what you notice while listening.

4. Do I alter my voice?

Describe what happens when you alter your voice. What happens when you raise or lower your voice? When you increase or decrease your speed? When you talk repetitively and when you pause to take a breath? Look for examples in daily life when you change your voice.

Rule Five

Pay attention to your breathing.

"Breathe deeply!" we tell someone who is under stress and has lost his sense of perspective. We know that breathing deeply is the most successful method for easing stress and reducing fear. We recognize this but often forget.

Breathing is not only the best cure for fear and stress management, it is also an opportunity to put yourself in another person's shoes, to feel things the way he does. If we examine the way the other person is breathing and imitate him for a short period of time, we can sense the way the other person is really feeling. This exercise enables us to experience compassion for another human being. Practicing breathing exercises and observing breathing patterns in others can be tried in short intervals throughout your day.

The following questions show how we can make others more accessible to us by observing our breathing while we interact with others:

◎ *How is the other person breathing, shallowly or deeply?*

◎ *Do I feel the need to adapt to her breathing rhythm or would I prefer to breathe against her breathing rhythm?*

◎ *Have I ever noticed that I could change a tense situation through one deep breath?*

If we examine the way the other person is breathing and imitate him for a short period of time, we can sense the way the other person is really feeling.

Exercises

1. *How do I breathe?*

Briefly observe your breathing by laying your hands first on your stomach, then on your rib cage, then on your chest and, finally, on your collarbone. What moves when you breathe deeply?

2. *When do I breathe consciously?*

Describe a few specific situations when you consciously noticed that you breathed deeply. For example, the beginning of a walk through the woods or when stretching the upper part of your body at your desk during a break or after a satisfying meal.

3. *I breathe with someone else in the same rhythm.*

Describe your experience when you breathe consciously in the same rhythm as a trusted person, such as a friend or a coworker, looking at this person while you breathe.

Rule Six

Be aware of timing.

"Timing" is a meaningful expression for anyone involved in sports, games, and theater. It describes the appropriateness of communication processes. The following questions clarify the importance of being aware of the right moment and the perfect time in a communication situation. Consider the following questions:

"Timing" is a meaningful expression for anyone involved in sports, games, and theater.

◎ *Do I give the other person enough time to speak his mind? Does my body language give him enough space to express what is on his mind?*

◎ *Do I give him time so he can understand my comment?*

◎ *Do I encourage the other person, with positive body language, to get to the point? Or does my stillness drive him to fearfully avoid the issue we are discussing?*

◎ *Am I consciously aware of how much I can influence another with my body language?*

◎ *Am I conscious of how much I can be manipulated by body language?*

◎ *Does my negative body language make me frantic and lead me to choose the wrong timing?*

◎ *Do I feel that I create enough space for what I want to tell the other person?*

◎ *Do I give myself enough time and space for the question and the answer?*

Exercises

1. *I observe myself during a conversation.*

Describe whether you react frantically or hesitantly in normal conversation. Are you nervous or calm?

2. *How do I behave when I get upset in a verbal encounter?*

Describe whether you become loud and aggressive or are quiet and withdrawn. Also, describe the habits of others in conversation that increase your anger, set you off in a rage, or make you withdrawn and shy.

3. I carry on a harmonious conversation.

Describe what conditions you and the other person need to have a harmonious and effective conversation.

Rule Seven

*Pay attention to the appropriateness
to the situation.*

This last of the *Seven Rules* doesn't apply to partners in communication but rather to our surroundings. In theater, the director would ask, "Do the set, costumes, and props all fit the scene?" With this rule, awareness should be directed toward the staging of the situation— the physical setting surrounding our world.

The following questions demonstrate that the staging of a communication situation begins long before the actual situation takes place. (Once again, because of the sensitive nature of these questions, they are to be directed to oneself and not to the other person. The methods we employ must adhere to the principle of compassion toward others.) Answer the following questions:

Do the set, costumes, and props all fit the scene?

- ◎ *Does my hairstyle suit me?*
- ◎ *Does my clothing complement my personality and the situation?*
- ◎ *Do the watch, eyeglasses, and rings that I wear enhance my appearance?*
- ◎ *What do I want to express with my clothing and style?*
- ◎ *Is the room appropriate for the conversation I want to have? How was the room specially prepared for what I want to accomplish?*

◎ *Have I checked the communication equipment before we started—the overhead projector, flip chart, lighting, video camera, and sound equipment?*

◎ *Have I considered the perfect seating arrangement for the table?*

◎ *Have I reflected upon what I want to offer during a conversation and, most importantly, in what stages I wish to offer it?*

◎ *Are the room, the purpose of the meeting, and I in an appropriate and harmonious relationship to one another?*

Exercises

Describe the type of person you would like to be and how you would change your figure, hair, clothing, and jewelry to become this person.

1. *What "type" am I?*

After looking at yourself in a large mirror, describe what clothing and jewelry you are wearing to create a certain impression.

2. *What type of person would I like to be?*

Describe the type of person you would like to be and how you would change your figure, hair, clothing, and jewelry to become this person. Be as vivid as possible. Describe physical details.

3. *How do I prepare for a conversation situation?*

Accurately describe, using specific examples, how you go about preparing the room and yourself for an important conversation. Do you concentrate on your breathing? Do you bring accessories or use props to enhance the atmosphere of the room?

Johannes Galli in *Communication Theater* for the Allianz Group.
This module of the Galli Method® is used for teambuilding processes.
It increases team orientation, strengthens the impromptu skills and
creates a wonderful atmosphere.

PHOTOGRAPH BY GEORG NEMEC

Course Examples

Chinese-German-American and American-German-Chinese

I had the great fortune to come in contact with different kinds of people during the four training sessions I gave to American-German-Chinese companies in China in 1998. They offered courses in the intercultural field and invited me to make a presentation.

I experienced profound insight regarding the differing forms of body language within the German, American, and Chinese cultures.

I specially prepared a training series entitled, *Intercultural Communication and Body Language.* It was a rewarding experience for me, as my work was well received by the participants in the People's Republic of China.

Three of these training sessions took place in Beijing (Peking), and the last in Shanghai. During the workshops, I experienced profound insight regarding the differing forms of body language within the German, American, and Chinese cultures.

I've made an effort to capture with words the occurrences during the courses. My documentation of this trip has come from a need to preserve this valuable treasure of experience.

China, 1998

Upon arriving at the airport in Beijing, I already regretted my preconceived perceptions from the German media, which had given me a completely different picture of the People's Republic of China. I didn't discover the image of the deeply depressed and oppressed Chinese that were constantly suffering from human rights violations. Instead I found strong, lively, and free-spirited people.

It was impossible to ignore the fact that many people living on the streets were struggling to survive but there was no doubt they would overcome the struggle and win in the end. I had been taught the Chinese built a country that had accomplished the oldest and highest cultural achievements in the world, and now sat around

Johannes Galli on his 1998 China tour, here in front of the Shanghai skyline.

PHOTOGRAPH BY GALLI ARCHIVES

on the side of the street in tents made of sacks, living from hand to mouth. I was accustomed to the idea that China was poor until I arrived and saw skyscrapers which, with their bold architecture, could compete with the monumental buildings in San Francisco, New York, or Los Angeles.

It's a well-known fact that the different body languages of the contrasting cultures of Europe, America, and China are the source of disastrous misunderstandings.

Guards stood sternly in front of important buildings and exuded ironclad discipline while on the street, not a single rule as prescribed by German traffic regulations was followed. Would the bike rider suddenly turn left without giving a signal or continue riding in the middle of the street? Why did a truck approach me from the right on an expressway? How did the taxi driver know that the truck coming from the right would stop? Because my senses became confused, there wasn't a single moment when I thought it might be possible for me to negotiate Chinese road traffic by myself.

At first, the Chinese seemed cold, rejecting, and unfriendly towards me. However, as soon as they had acquired my trust, they bubbled over with cheerfulness. And, of course, my brave attempts to speak the Chinese language gave them much cause for laughter.

The goal of the courses I presented at various businesses was to convey the differences in the German and Chinese body language by using the Galli Method. I quickly became aware of their need for my training. It's a well-known fact that the different body languages of the contrasting cultures of Europe, America, and China are the source of disastrous misunderstandings. Since misunderstandings can poison the atmosphere at work, it was refreshing for the participants to be offered playful possibilities for finding solutions that encouraged the understanding of foreign cultures.

China, thousands of years old with a culture steeped in tradition, had been shaken by profound political changes and torn into a thousand pieces. This provided an opportunity for a fundamental transformation. In the twenty-first century, China is the giant who is awakening slowly, growing conscious of its own strength. "If there is a Zeitgeist that sweeps around the world creating new eras, then it is currently in the People's Republic of China." This was my first impression of China, which was quoted in an article in the *Galli News* 3/1999. It expresses the passion I felt for this country.

To familiarize the reader with a culture as foreign as that of the Chinese, I would like to share a list of impressions I accumulated while visiting China:

I had barely landed at the airport in Beijing when I immediately ran into trouble. Naïvely, I hadn't bothered to secure a visa or an invitation from a recognized Chinese institution. The woman at the entry office shook her head but I sensed I was welcome in her country. She sent me to the passport department where they took care of everything, except the photograph. She then sent me to a room where a friendly young Chinese woman would take my picture. I smiled twelve times with what was, I imagined, a flattering facial expression. But the camera wasn't working. As a German, if I were the photographer, I would have expressed frustration and a grinding of teeth at such an inconvenient failure. Her smile, which almost turned into laughter at the continued failures, irritated me. Was she laughing at me? In a later training session, I discovered the answer . . . .

At the beginning of my trip, I had thought that I would communicate effectively with English, but soon realized that I would be lost without a translator. Essential activities such as shopping, ordering food, and riding taxis would not have been possible without him. Gradually, I learned to interpret his reactions when I had done something wrong. I clearly remember a festive meal at a big round table, as is common in China, where I asked a pregnant woman at the table if she was giving birth to her first child. My translator winced and later explained that it was a silly question because couples who live in the city in China are generally only allowed

Her smile, which almost turned into laughter at the continued failures, irritated me. Was she laughing at me?

to have one child. And, I was surprised when a taxi driver did not want to drive us from Beijing to a suburb forty minutes away because it was "too far".

During my stay in Beijing, I lived in a temple adjoining a hotel. I spent hours in deep conversation with my translator, Dr. Xu Tianxiang, about the different perceptions of European, American, and Chinese service. My desire to eat breakfast at 8:00 a.m. was rejected. It was considered too early. When the housekeeper, waiter, and cook spoke to one another in loud voices late at night in front of my hotel room, I politely asked my translator if he could do something about it. He replied that the Chinese enjoy being together and assume that others also enjoy their presence. In addition, when ordering meals in restaurants, it seemed that one dish was always forgotten, as if it was polite to be imperfect.

Johannes Galli and his Chinese translator, Dr. Xu Tianxiang, in Beijing.

PHOTOGRAPH BY GALLI ARCHIVES

I was amazed when a monk who, at the end of a long and intense discussion about Buddhism, Taoism, and Confucianism, showed me a newspaper article in which the Communist party declared that Buddhism was good for restoring morals and health. It made me realize that the oldest traditional religion in China was also struggling for recognition.

The following are the four training courses I carried out during my stay in the People's Republic of China. I hope that by sharing them it will give you the opportunity of deepening your own intercultural experiences.

Training Courses

The First Training

The first training session took place on October 9, 1998, in the Center for Integrated Agricultural Development (CIAD) at the China Agricultural University in Beijing, People's Republic of China.

In China, there are a lot of questions to clarify before the scene can begin.

Fifteen participants, including professors, students, and secretaries were present. With the exception of one American professor, they were all Chinese between the ages 25 and 50. They all had a connection to Americans and to America and the training was held in English.

After a short introduction, in which I introduced myself and my method, we immediately developed scenes to act out, which were intended to illustrate cultural differences in body language.

◉ *Two work colleagues meet each other in the hall.*

I immediately noticed a difference between this and the same body language training session I had facilitated in Germany. The participants wanted to know the exact relationship between the two colleagues and demanded elaborate details. It was clear that they viewed it within the framework of a very complex system. Were the colleagues acquaintances, friends, or did they only work together?

In a training course in Germany, if the suggestion is made to act out a chance meeting with the boss in the hall, the two participants rise from their chairs and begin. They carry a very clear picture of what a boss is. In China, there are a lot of questions to clarify before the scene can begin. Is the boss nice? Have you not seen each other for a long time? Is the boss returning from vacation? What kind of relationship does the boss have with his employees in general and individually?

During these scenes, the difference between the Chinese and German body language clearly emerged.

The Chinese person held his or her body in a controlled manner and barely moved. Even their hands, which normally move naturally during speech, were concealed behind their backs. This was in contrast to exchanges that alternated between a still, impenetrable look and a spontaneous smile. The composed stance made it difficult to recognize what the Chinese person really experienced and thought. The basic Chinese principle that others are, for polite reasons, not to be burdened with one's feelings, could clearly be sensed.

During the assessment that followed this scene, I used the term "reduced body language" in association with Chinese body language and immediately sensed that the Chinese felt harshly criticized. I noticed a sensitivity on their part that later prevented me from speaking in clear and direct terms. I immediately took the time to explain that *body language is neither good nor bad, but simply is.*

Body language is neither good nor bad, but simply is.

◉ *Boss returns from a seven-week stay in a foreign country and visits his employee in his or her office.*

The participants determined the details of the next scene to be acted out. The employee is sitting at the computer when the boss enters the room. Both actors were making an effort to create a warm exchange. The boss even laid his hand on his employee's shoulder. As I witnessed the scene, I sensed that the players were forcing themselves to appear to be getting along.

Everyone was still a bit offended by my remark about "reduced body language". I then involved the participants in a passionate discussion about what in an individual's body language is caused by personal history and what elements we acquire from our cultural background.

During this discussion, I sensed a wound that was connected to the huge political changes China had experienced during the last 50 years. China had still been traditionally structured at the beginning of the twentieth

A break in the Galli Training *Improving Your Personal Effectiveness* for international managers of Arthur D. Little International.

century, but this foundation suddenly changed with the communist transformation of the country. Since the Cultural Revolution, it had been unacceptable and outdated to practice original traditions. Following the Cultural Revolution, the rural proletarian approach to living had been more desirable and revered.

◉ The flirt scene

As I didn't feel comfortable in my knowledge of this political domain, I suggested that a scene be acted out in which a typical Chinese flirt scene is enacted. This idea was received with much enthusiasm. One 30 year-old professor was motivated to enact this scene because he was single. He suggested the following situation: He begins to talk to a young lady at the bus station and later continues the conversation on the bus. While sitting together, the bus stops at several stations. The actors wanted to act out the entire scene in Chinese, which I encouraged them to do. The goal of the man was to arrange a date with the woman. Would he be successful?

The scene was over. All the participants were laughing, grinning, and clapping. And then came the big question.

As soon as they both stepped on the stage, he spoke to the woman and the scene began. He smiled and asked a question and she smiled and answered. Then the "bus" came. The American professor strategically placed two chairs on the stage so that the scene could continue. The players entered the "bus" and sat down next to each other. He said something and she smiled and replied and he smiled and asked something else and she smiled and replied again. Then the "bus" came to a stop and it was time to exit. They bowed to each other and said good-bye in a friendly manner.

The scene was over. All the participants were laughing, grinning, and clapping. And then came the big question.

The participants looked at me expectantly as a young woman anxiously asked me, "What do you think, did he manage it? Did he arrange a date with her?"

With all the superiority and authority of someone who is used to observing body language, I said, "Of course he did. He asked her out on a date. They're going to see each other again soon."

Laughter filled the room. Everyone was bent over in their chairs laughing—except me. I was completely perplexed.

We talked for a long time about my false assessment of the situation. The only thing I could say in my defense was that, if a woman in Germany laughs and smiles that much during a conversation with a man she doesn't know very well, she's unlikely to turn down a date.

I convincingly showed the participants how hurtful this situation could be for a German man. After having such a friendly conversation with a Chinese woman, he would be convinced that he would receive a "yes" to a further rendezvous but then, much to his surprise, he received an extremely bitter "no".

It became clear to everyone in the room how important it is to improve mutual understanding in order to prevent the hurt that can be caused by cultural misunderstanding.

It became clear to everyone in the room how important it is to improve mutual understanding in order to prevent the hurt that can be caused by cultural misunderstandings.

In the feedback that followed, everyone seemed to be moved and amazed by how strongly we perceive each other through body language.

Constructive Criticism

Along with much positive feedback, I was also given constructive criticism. I should have described the scene to be enacted more precisely. When I included extensive details in my presentation, the participants were amazed by the penetrating effect of the three-hour training session and were delighted by the lively method. They were all used to highly focused detail-oriented teaching by other Germans who stood at the front of the room in one unmoving position.

Conclusion

Throughout the three-hour training session, I also noticed that there was constant coming and going. Each of the participants had gotten up two or three times to pour more hot water in their tea or to go to the bathroom. When I questioned the meaning of this activity, I was assured that this was absolutely normal—by Chinese standards the training session had been a highly successful gathering.

At the end of the session, I observed a woman who looked at me with embarrassment, looked away, then returned her gaze. When I looked at her questioningly, she said she had no idea how to act toward me now that she was not allowed to smile too much. (During our conversation she gave me an extraordinarily friendly smile, which I refrained from interpreting in my typical German way.)

I explained to her and to the others standing around listening that it was not my intention to teach intellectual control of body language but rather conscious observation of the effect it has on ourselves and others.

It was not my intention to teach intellectual control of body language but rather conscious observation of the effect it has on ourselves and others.

I felt confirmed in my convictions when each of the participants let me know that the training had been refreshing, moving, and had given them cause for reflection. I was relieved and pleased by the success of the experience for both the participants and me.

Exercises

1. *What differences between the body language of foreign cultures and my own have I noticed?*

Describe, on the basis of your experiences during vacations or business trips, how you perceived the forms of body language in foreign cultures. Using several examples and as accurately as possible, describe the body language characteristics that are foreign to you.

2. *A misunderstanding has occurred.*

Describe how a misunderstanding occurred because you wrongly interpreted body language in a culture that was foreign to you.

3. *Another misunderstanding has occurred.*

Describe how your interaction with another came to a misunderstanding because you used body language that was misinterpreted in the culture that is foreign to you.

4. *I smiled in a friendly way because I thought I had to smile in a friendly way.*

Describe a situation that became complicated because you smiled and your smile was misunderstood.

Describe a situation that became complicated because you smiled and your smile was misunderstood.

5. *I was smiled at in a friendly way and I came to conclusions.*

Describe how you were smiled at in a foreign country, what conclusions you came to, how the situation developed further or how you ended the exchange.

The Second Training

The second training session took place on October 13, 1998. It was announced as an "open training" in Beijing and was held in English. The participants included the German executive manager of a well-known German electronics firm, two Chinese professors from the CIAD, one doctor, and one doctorate candidate who had spontaneously signed up for another session, an American woman from the American chamber of commerce in Beijing, and a German language teacher with her students from the German Foreign Academy in Beijing.

From the very beginning, it was clear that this training would not be as lively and amusing as the first training because the participants didn't know one another. The seven Chinese language students' English was not always proficient and the older participants seemed to be somewhat dissatisfied with the unbalanced arrangement of the participants.

Despite these difficulties, this session turned out to be enormously creative and amusing after the initial rough beginning.

◉ The job interview

For the first topic, the students wanted to reenact "The job interview". This scene was quickly set up because all that was needed were two chairs facing each other. Two language students acted out the situation. One played the boss and the other played the applicant who wanted a position. The "boss" sat very relaxed on the chair while the "applicant" sat straight and stiff at the edge of the chair and nervously played with her fingers. With these two players it was easy to observe the interplay between physical and inner poise. My suggestion to the woman looking for work, to breathe in deeply to ease her nervousness, was wholeheartedly accepted. As soon as the "applicant" began to breathe in her own rhythm, independently from the "boss", she became visibly relaxed. This resulted in her transformation. She became more confident and substantially more competent than could have been assumed at the beginning of the job interview. Soon there was no question that the "boss" would hire the self-confident and competent "applicant".

It was a very effective scene in which additional support was given with which the actor corrected the performance, resulting in a positive change. This was an extremely successful start because everyone was impressed with how a small correction to the flow of breathing could change an entire impression.

A small correction to the flow of breathing could change an entire impression.

◉ The boss gives a task

For the next scene, the potential for conflict between a German boss and a Chinese assistant was chosen as the basis.

Mrs. N., the woman from the American Chamber of Commerce, served as the boss of the Chinese assistant. She gave her a complicated copying task, "copy only half of page 62, switch the lower two lines on page 63 with the upper two lines on page 59, and then copy the pages and prepare them to be submitted."

The "assistant", who could not follow the instructions from her "boss", reacted as expected. With politely concealed insecurity, she nodded and smiled although she had not understood the task. She gave the impression, however, that she had understood everything.

I used this scene to illustrate how much time and money is wasted (not only in Chinese offices) when, out of fear and insecurity, coworkers try to give the impression that they have understood the required task without having understood it at all.

I suggested to the "boss" that she check back more often and confirm whether the "assistant" has completely understood the task. I then advised the "assistant" to express the truth and not fake understanding. The American, Mrs. N., and the Chinese assistant considered my advice and, during a repeat performance of the scene, successfully applied these simple changes.

The Chinese "assistant" was able to maintain her dignity as she forced herself to ask questions when she had not understood something. The "boss" did not appear arrogant, as was feared, when she repeatedly checked to see if her "assistant" had correctly understood her instructions. The effect was efficient and compassionate.

If we expose the lack of communication as it is happening, we can solve problems as they occur.

The audience watching the scene sat silently impressed. Because the scenes were acted out enthusiastically, I reiterated that if we expose the lack of communication as it is happening, we can solve problems as they occur.

◉ *Introduction of names*

The next scene dealt with the subject of introducing names. This is always a delicate point because one often does not understand how to pronounce the other person's name and doesn't dare ask for fear of appearing impolite. The fear is that the other person will believe that no one had been listening when they shared their name.

I have often noticed that people with difficult or unusual names, instead of speaking them slowly and clearly so that the other person will be able to understand, speak them quietly and quickly in order to conceal the difficulty of the pronunciation. Oftentimes, we would like to save the other person the effort of having to learn our names. Nevertheless, the fact was that the Germans and the Americans did not correctly understand the Chinese names and the Chinese did not correctly understand the American and the German names. This is a very unpleasant situation. One would like to address the other by name because it creates a personal and trusting atmosphere but one is afraid to offend the other by addressing him or her by the wrong name.

In one scene, I asked the participants to pay attention when they introduced themselves by clearly expressing their names. They met each other at a champagne reception, introduced themselves, and chatted about their lives in the relaxed atmosphere. It was fascinating to observe the charming effect the truth can create. Everyone who had not spoken his or her name clearly and had not been understood by the other person, repeated it until the other could pronounce it correctly. They had fun experiencing a first greeting that was not considered "small talk" but rather that the initial energy was spent learning the correct pronunciation of names.

It was fascinating to observe the charming effect the truth can create.

At the time, I used this exercise to examine differences in American, German, and Chinese physical distances. Distinctive differences were apparent. While the distance between two bodies during a conversation

Metamorphosis of The Butterfly, a Galli Business Theater piece focusing on change management within the Siemens Company.

in American culture is slightly less than an arm's length, as it also is in German culture, it was between ten and twenty centimeters more for the Chinese who consider the greater distance more pleasant and polite.

After observing this occurrence, Mr. R. said, "This is very surprising for me because what I've noticed in China is that, if I, for example, sit on the ground in a park to have a rest, a Chinese person who passes by me does not avoid me as I am used to in Germany. Instead the Chinese person walks much more closely to me."

Excited and somewhat irritated, Mrs. N. added, "They will disrespectfully sit down right next to you on a field."

Mr. R. continued, "Once I spread my towel on a mile-long empty beach and was enjoying this relaxing solitude and, minutes later, a few Chinese people came and lay down right next to me."

In order to reconcile these two seemingly contradictory phenomena, we decided that, during a confrontation, the Chinese preferred more distance than Americans and Germans. Yet, when interacting socially, they don't accept the American and German rules of physical distance; rather, they desire greater nearness.

For Germans, I was certain that this unusual behavior concealed a different mental attitude. I was to be proven right because a Chinese woman explained that a Chinese family normally feels sorry for somebody sitting alone and tries to relieve the loneliness with their nearness. It's as if the Chinese person thinks, *Oh look, there's a foreigner. He has no wife and no children, the poor man. Come, let's sit next to him so he won't feel his loneliness as strongly because he'll have us near him to ease his sadness.*

He was a 30 year-old bachelor and, for understandable reasons, was very interested in gathering experience on how to approach the female sex in this foreign country.

Mr. R. became eager to participate in this scene because he suspected that my method could save him a great deal of unpleasantness. He was a 30 year-old bachelor and, for understandable reasons, was very interested in gathering experience on how to approach the female sex in this foreign country.

◉ The date

We quickly agreed on the following scene: Mr. R. wanted to call a young Chinese woman on the phone and invite her to go to visit the Forbidden City. Using pantomime, the two acted out a "telephone call" by placing their thumbs against their ears and their pinkies to their mouths. Over and over, she laughed politely and turned him down with the explanation that she did not have any time. Unwilling to give up and unable to accept "no" as an answer, Mr. R. said he would call her again.

In order to force a clear decision from the Chinese woman, I intervened and said that the young woman had free time this afternoon. They both acted out the following scenario through conversation:

After Mr. R. charmingly asked her out, she said she could not come because she might have an appointment.

I laughed and asked her what she meant by the statement, "I might have an appointment." Embarrassed, the Chinese woman explained to me her predicament. Because of her moral upbringing she was forbidden to go out with a strange man right after the first phone call. She was also taught not to lie and she was not allowed to hurt a strange man. These three issues caused her to reply with the awkward and ambiguous response, "I might have an appointment."

The response, although not entirely truthful, is created so as not to hurt the other person's feelings.

Everyone in the group saw my reaction to her answer and was now eager to know how a German woman would behave in such a situation.

Trying to be as truthful as possible, I answered according to my own experience. A German woman in such a situation would not necessarily feel bound to tell the truth and might say, "It's too bad I can't go with you to the Forbidden City because at three o'clock, I'm playing tennis with a friend." I further explained the German word: *Notlüge*, a word which means "white lie". The response, although not entirely truthful, is created so as not to hurt the other person's feelings.

During the break, I was surrounded by the young language school students who were desperate to know why the German men they had had contact with in their exchange program always asked them the same questions, "What's your name? How old are you? What are your hobbies? Do you have a boyfriend?"

I then asked how a Chinese man would approach a woman and they answered, "He would ask polite questions which would create an atmosphere of trust. He would never ask directly!"

◉ The giving of gifts

After the break, we continued with a scene of an older German woman's problem. She told us that she often felt hurt during visits when the gift she had chosen with care and effort was placed aside by the host. I didn't want to believe this and suspected that the woman was, perhaps, too sensitive, but the following scene taught me to see her concern in a different light.

In this scene, the woman visited a Chinese woman who was the same age. She had obviously been invited to dinner and held a tastefully gift-wrapped book in her hands. The receiver of the gift simply glanced at it, set it aside, and immediately changed the subject.

Everyone in the room nodded in agreement; the Chinese, the Germans and the American confirmed that this situation was typical. They had encountered the same situation. The German woman claimed that she felt very hurt by such cool behavior and interpreted it as rejection.

Through questioning, I took the time to find out what the hidden mentality was behind this behavior. I knew from experience that only an understanding of the different belief systems could clear up the misunderstanding resulting from drastic differences in body language.

Only an understanding of the different belief systems could clear up the misunderstanding resulting from drastic differences in body language.

The German wanted to be rewarded for her efforts in choosing the gift and wanted feedback so she would know whether or not she had made the right choice. She searched for a sign to see if she had correctly judged the character of the Chinese woman—was she being rude or was something else going on? She desperately wanted recognition and praise for her efforts in trying to please her host.

The Chinese woman, however, was raised to be reserved and had placed the gift aside and quickly changed the subject so that she would not give the impression that she was too eager to receive the gift.

All the Chinese people in the room confirmed, with heavy nodding, that gifts were under no circumstances to be opened in the presence of the gift-giver. This ritual happens later, when the guest has already left. The Chinese custom is to make certain that the guest does not receive the impression that one is greedy for gifts.

◉ Different body language habits

Toward the end of the training session, a heavy argument developed between the participants. A very bright Chinese woman from the south asked me why German professors often take off their eyeglasses during a discussion or a talk and then put them back on or put them in their mouths. The question amused the other Chinese people in the room.

It is ridiculous to try to find what is "good" behavior and what is "bad" behavior during communication – the point is to find out why things happen.

I explained that Germans believe it is a sign of concentration to forget the body and focus on the mind. The Chinese people couldn't believe this. The situation escalated when the young Chinese girls laughed about the fact that Germans loudly blow their noses in public and then even stick their tissues in their pockets.

The American, Mrs. N. asked, "Is blowing your nose worse than spitting on the street or loudly smacking your lips while eating and then burping like I have seen so often here in China?"

During the heated debate, I again explained that it is ridiculous to try to find out what is "good" and what is "bad" behavior during communication—the point is to find out why things happen.

For the Chinese, smacking your lips and burping conveys how *good* the food tastes. They see it as praise and recognition for the host and the cook.

We couldn't explain why Germans think nothing about blowing their noses in public. And yet, they expressed that they found the spitting of the Chinese people impolite and annoying.

For the Chinese, smacking your lips and burping conveys how good the food tastes.

The feedback that followed was constructive and each participant shared, which body language expressions could be taken home to further develop the ability to understand others better.

Exercises

1. *How do I act when I haven't correctly understood the name of the other person or I pronounced it incorrectly?*

   Describe, using actual experiences, what strategy you use when you have not understood the name of the other person or have pronounced it incorrectly?

2. *How do I act when the other person has not correctly understood my name or pronounces it incorrectly?*

   Describe, using actual experiences, how you act when the other person has not correctly understood your name or has mispronounced it.

3. *How do you perceive the usual distance between people in foreign cultures?*

   Describe, on the basis of your experiences on vacation or on business trips, which distance between people you perceived to be comfortable, too close, or too distant.

4. *Which forms of body language in foreign cultures have seemed strange to you?*

   Describe, on the basis of your experiences on vacation or business trips, which forms of body language seemed strange to you and which forms of *your* body language seemed strange to others.

The Third Training

The Deputy Department Manager of Human Resources for a large international German chemical company booked the workshop, *Intercultural Communication and Body Language*. The training took place in the Jing Guang Center in Beijing and was held in English.

Mid- and high-level managers participated: a Chinese and a German executive manager, two American mid-level managers, a younger Chinese mid-level manager, an older Chinese executive assistant, two German assistant managers, a Chinese veterinarian, and a Chinese doctorate candidate in economics.

Awareness of one's own body language and that of colleagues makes work processes more fluid, intense, and effective.

After a general introduction, in which I pointed out that the awareness of one's own body language and that of colleagues makes work processes more fluid, intense, and effective, I demonstrated a few basic forms of body language. I discussed the *Seven Rules for Effective Communication* that I had published in my book *Body Language and Communication.* (At that time, an English translation of this book was not available.)

My introductory synopsis and demonstrations were necessary and helped to break the cold and untrusting atmosphere in the room. At the beginning, I was confronted with the typical managerial attitude, "What does he know that we don't?"

After orchestrating a few breathing exercises together to enable them to get in touch with their own breath, an atmosphere of trust and comfort arose and we were finally able to get down to the business at hand. In accordance with my method, I asked the participants to formulate situations from their daily business lives that they wanted to improve.

◉ *Public speaking*

One of the young Americans briskly announced that he would go first and we immediately developed a scene that was suitable for him because he wanted help to improving his performance as a lecturer. He spontaneously gave a speech in which he recommended the goals of the company he represented to a somewhat interested audience.

In the feedback that followed, he expected to receive a response from me that consisted of key principles he could incorporate into his lecture to improve its effect on the audience. As expected, he precisely described who he felt supported him and who he was certain rejected him by interpreting their gazes and body language.

I then formulated my suggestion: During the speech, be aware of those who are supporting you with an open body posture and an open look and do not try, as it often unconsciously happens, to "engage" listeners who have displayed their rejection of your speech with closed body postures and empty stares.

I had often observed that lecturers became insecure by focusing on listeners who displayed complete rejection.

Over the years, during workshops and consultations, I had often observed that lecturers became insecure by

Galli Situational Theater, another module of the Galli Business Theater, changes the training into an interactive process. Managers of the Dow Chemical Company worked on an effective presentation in interactive scenes.

PHOTOGRAPH BY GALLI ARCHIVES

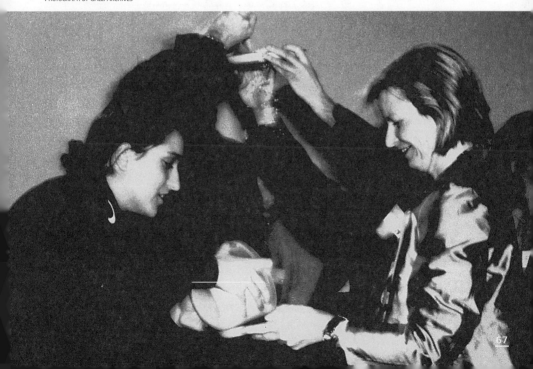

67

focusing on listeners who displayed complete rejection. I'm familiar with this occurrence from talks and lectures that I have presented, as well as from my stage appearances as an actor. Those who reject your words or your stage presence are known as "opponents"—they always exist in the audience.

When the speaker, consciously or unconsciously, tries to convince this "opponent", he falls into dependence on the reaction of this member of the audience and gradually loses those who had been receptive to him. Performing for the "opponent" escalates, as the speaker loses more and more power and delivers a bad performance. The final outcome—the lecturer fulfills the vision of his "opponent".

In a repetition of the lecture, the young American tried, with success, to embrace this suggestion and orient himself only to his "friends" in the audience and ignore his "enemies". In this way, he eventually relaxed because he didn't have to exert strenuous energy convincing a nonbeliever. No longer battling to convert the "opponent", the young American performed with ease.

The more relaxed you stand in front of your audience, the more successfully and effectively you can express what you want to convey.

◎ *Sales presentations*

The more relaxed you stand in front of your audience, the more successfully and effectively you can express what you want to convey.

To explain this theory, I told the participants about an experiment I carried out with German sales trainers. The participants in the training had to first give a talk about a business subject and directly afterward speak about the topic, "How I relax from my stress at work". It was amazing and impressive to witness the enormous difference in quality between the "business talk" and the "relaxation talk".

The business talks were stiff, strenuous, and energy-draining, whereas, during the "relaxing topic", the participants seemed to almost overflow with physical poise, effectiveness, confidence in presentation, power to persuade, and cleverness. Everyone in the audience agreed that being relaxed gave the impression that the speaker was a professional and an expert in their field and was truly enthusiastic about the subject they were sharing.

After this initial success and the gratitude of the American, the path was set for further success of the training.

◉ *During a speech*

The Chinese executive manager asked me what was better, to stand and deliver a speech from behind a podium or to stand and speak directly in front of the audience without any kind of barrier between himself and the audience. I answered his question frankly, "If you don't like to hide your body behind a podium and don't need anything to hold onto, then it is naturally an advantage to present yourself openly in front of the audience. If you present your "whole" self, then you can reach the "whole" audience. If you would rather not openly and freely present yourself, you are better off having a barrier you can stand behind to hide your insecurities."

◉ *Language to use during a speech*

A young Chinese man wanted to present a small speech in his field of expertise because he, too, was responsible for giving lectures and wanted to improve his presentation skills. I suggested he deliver the first part of the talk in his mother tongue, Chinese, and the second part in the business language, English.

If you present your "whole" self, then you can reach the "whole" audience.

During the Chinese portion of the talk, he stood stiff as a rod in front of his audience with his hands placed at his sides. Consciously or unconsciously, he followed the Chinese ideal of creating a dignified impression by presenting himself completely controlled and still.

At my request, he continued his speech in English and what I expected, happened, completely surprising the others. His body language suddenly became effective. He moved his hands from his sides and, with quick gestures, supported and emphasized what he was verbalizing. He took a few steps forward and moved around the room. Everyone was surprised to see how the spirit of a language could influence body language.

Everyone was surprised to see how the spirit of a language could influence body language.

This gave me the opportunity to explain how pictures in the imagination can determine body language. I advised the young Chinese man to always take into consideration what is most useful for him. For example, to give his speech in the traditional Chinese style or the modern Western style. He politely thanked me and expressed to all the others that he had just had quite a revealing experience.

◉ Emotions in the workplace

Then a young Chinese woman told us about her problem in brief, but emotional, words. She didn't know how to calm her boss down because when he was angry with her and began to scold her, his scolding, no matter what she did, always got louder and more furious. A skit for this topic had already occurred to me and I asked one of the American managers if he would be willing to play the hot-tempered boss. He replied with a wink, "I would love to!" He and the Chinese woman rose from their chairs and began.

The American manager started in on her right away. Immediately following his first angry remark, the Chinese woman reacted with genuine shock and, what did she do? She smiled.

Of course, the boss didn't feel that he was being taken seriously and increased his method of expression. His volume and gestures became intensified, which led to a broader smile from the Chinese woman. (I was baffled and couldn't comprehend the woman's response.) They repeated the whole incident again and then both discontinued the scene because it had become clear to them and to the others that they had been witnesses to a dreadful misunderstanding.

Chinese people cope with failure by smiling. The smile is meant to conceal the strong emotions with which others and, above all, a boss shouldn't be burdened. While Europeans and Americans expect some gesture of humility or clear body language showing repentance from someone who has made a mistake, the Chinese person conceals the inner shock behind a smiling mask.

At this point, my summary, pleading for the necessity of these kinds of training sessions, was received with enthusiastic applause.

◎ Posturing while giving and receiving tasks

The German executive manager, who had loosened up toward the end of the session, initiated the final scene in this training. He said he felt that his habit of sitting relaxed in a chair was met with little understanding, and even rejection, by Chinese people. He wanted to use this opportunity to know if his feeling was correct.

We placed two chairs in the middle of the room we had previously defined as the "stage". The chair with arms was where the boss sat and the chair without arms was the assistant's chair. We would observe how the boss and the assistant communicated.

The scene began. The German sank down in his chair, slouched over the arm and, from this crouched position, gave his assistant, who sat bolt upright at the edge of the chair, a task to complete.

After the Chinese woman had looked at me helplessly several times, I carefully interrupted the scene and politely asked how they were each feeling at the moment. Before the Chinese woman could answer, the German said, "Wonderful, just like in real life." But then the Chinese woman spoke with indignation. *For her the boss showed no sign of managerial dignity and she felt hurt by his lack of respect.* Once again, I related how the openness of my method of acting out scenes allowed the disadvantaged person, in this case the Chinese woman, a new experience—to be able to talk freely and openly to her boss. I then explained to her that the "open" body language of the boss and his quick gestures while ordering the task was meant to motivate her to complete the assignment. After my explanation, she looked at me amazed and said, "An order is an order."

At this moment, two mentalities clashed—the traditional Chinese, which is hierarchical, and the European and the American, which are motivation-oriented. Instinctively, the highly useless discussion of which culture is "better" ensued. Acting as the moderator, ended this discussion with a compromise. The first priority has to be a desire to understand foreign cultures. At the conclusion of this workshop, all participants gave me enthusiastic words of thanks.

The first priority has to be a desire to understand foreign cultures.

◉ *Talk to your boss*

I was ready to leave the room when the Chinese executive assistant hesitantly approached me. She thanked me and told me that arguments between herself and her boss, which she had tried to calm with a smile,

Technology Driven—international businesses like DaimlerChrysler, BMW, and Audi love business theater presentations of the Galli Group. Lively product presentations are much more effective than regular presentations and speeches.

PHOTOGRAPH BY AXL JANSEN FOR LUFTHANSA MOAGAZINE

had often escalated and she now understood why. She then told me, "I never know, when my working hours are over and I can go home, whether I should say good-bye to my boss or just leave and not bother him." I told her, "There are certain times, when there is contact between people from two different cultures, where there are strict rules. If your boss is open-minded, then he would be pleased by a good-bye. If he is more reserved, then it would be better to simply leave." I continued, "I know that this isn't a satisfying answer but my advice to you is—talk to your boss! The new wave of the future in all companies now makes it possible to speak openly and exchange points of view. This is how agreements can be made, which both sides honor and misunderstandings are eliminated."

The new wave of the future in all companies now makes it possible to speak openly and exchange points of view.

Conclusion

During the delicious Chinese meal that followed, to which the manager of human resources invited me, we discussed the training. The manager told me he had received feedback from the others while I had been talking to the Chinese woman. All of the participants, without exception, had felt that they had learned more about Chinese, American and German living and working habits in those three hours than they had during their entire visits to China, America or Germany.

The gratitude of the manager manifested itself in an opulent Chinese meal, which familiarized me with the exquisiteness of the Chinese cuisine.

Exercises

1. *How do I differentiate between a "friend" and an "opponent" when giving a lecture?*

Describe how, on the basis of body language, you notice a "friend" or an "opponent" while giving a lecture. Explain whether you usually try to increase your number of "friends" by "getting them on your side," or whether you try to reduce your number of "opponents" by trying to convince them of your ideas.

2. *How does my body language change when speaking different languages?*

Describe how your body language changes when you speak in a foreign language, in the manner of your childhood, or when you speak perfect English (or your first language).

3. *I give a short report on a subject and then talk about my hobby.*

Describe how you felt during the report on the subject and how you felt when you talked about your hobby. Which changes in body language did you notice?

The Fourth Training

The manager for training and development of an internationally well-known synthetics and pharmaceuticals company from Germany had extended an invitation for my services. The training took place in the Hau Run Technology building in Shanghai.

There were seventeen participants. The majority were executive and mid-level managers of the German company, who were of American, German, and Chinese nationalities, as well as an American doctor of economics.

Similar to my last training, a detailed demonstration of my observations of body language was necessary to loosen up the reserved audience.

All of the Chinese participants spoke excellent English, so the training could be held in English without any problem. Similar to my last training, a detailed demonstration of my observations of body language was necessary to loosen up the reserved audience. In order to create a comfortable and trusting environment, this preliminary demonstration served to encourage open-mindedness because the topic of body language is personal and viewed cautiously and, oftentimes, mistrustfully.

◎ *Physical distance between coworkers*

I was very pleased when an Chinese woman shared a problem with us that she desperately wanted to solve. She described how the strange behavior of her boss spoiled her and her Chinese colleagues' enjoyment of the work. Her German boss had the habit of coming too close to her. Even when she moved out of the way, the boss came still closer until the proximity became unbearable for her. In addition, lately her Chinese co-worker had often been close to tears because she didn't know how to defend herself against so much German obtrusiveness. As previously stated, the normal distance between people in China is about ten to twenty centimeters more than in Germany or America (see "The Second Training" chapter).

The normal distance between people in China is about ten to twenty centimeters more than in Germany or America.

Furthermore, the young woman reported she had accompanied her boss, who worked for a Swabian bank, on a delegation trip to China and had noticed during the trip that many officials had given her helpless looks because the German had been standing too close to *them*. I naturally used this situation to point out the need for communication in the area of body language. Everyone was aware of the fact that, especially with regard to monetary negotiations where trust plays a key role, misunderstandings can have disastrous consequences.

During the scene, the woman who had initiated the exercise reached her limits. Perhaps it was because of the obtrusive player who constantly came too close to her or the memory of the torturous past weeks she had endured traveling with her boss. In any case, the young Chinese manager showed clear signs of stress after a few minutes into the exercise. As hard as she tried, she couldn't continue with the scene.

This wasn't a problem. I suggested she sit down, relax, and watch the rest of the scene. While another pair acted out the exercise, she sat away from the stage where she could observe the escalation of the problem from a secure and safe distance. By separating herself from the source of her frustration, it was possible for us to continue working through this exciting body language situation without further unsettling the nerves of the manager.

The second woman in the skit, who replaced her in a similar situation, was a teacher. For the masculine managerial part, we chose the role of a director whom, during a brief work-oriented talk with the woman, moved closer and closer to his colleague.

The teacher wanted to "hint" to her boss that he was invading her space. An amusing game began because the more the teacher hinted, the less the director noticed. He assumed her hints were directed toward everyone else but him. The teacher was verbally unsuccessful but non-verbally successful. She used body language full of gestures to keep the director at bay.

The teacher was verbally unsuccessful but non-verbally successful.

In the discussion that followed the scene, the young manager who had initiated the scene said that the exercise had made everything crystal clear. She learned by watching how the teacher had been successful in keeping the director at a distance by using a number of expansive gestures. With bright red cheeks and obviously happy, she thanked both players for helping her come to the realization that she can achieve her desired distance through gesturing.

◎ *Greeting coworkers*

After this skit, we took a break and then devoted ourselves to the discussion of European-American-Chinese greeting rituals. The Germans desperately wanted to know if shaking hands was an acceptable greeting for the Chinese. The Germans confessed they did not always feel comfortable doing this because the hand of the Chinese partner often felt too limp or too stiff while shaking hands.

The Chinese manager interjected, "Since the Cultural Revolution (1966), the traditional values in China have disappeared but alternatives have not be developed. In the old Chinese tradition, shaking hands was unthinkable. A verbal greeting with a slight nodding of the head and a straight body or the loose laying of the fisted hand in front of the heart were the traditional greeting forms." Then he said something that really attracted the attention of the German participants, "Usually we only shake hands at official occasions, never with friends." Surprised by this comment a German manager said, "And I thought that shaking hands was the expression of warm friendship in China!"

"Usually we only shake hands at official occasions, never with friends."

Being a witness to a great deal of insecurity concerning how Chinese, Americans, and Germans should greet one another, I asked the two Chinese people to act out three situations:

In the first situation, two Chinese strangers meet. One asks the other what time it is, the other person tells her and then they part. In the second situation, two school friends who have not seen each other in a long time, bump into each other. They recognize each other from their past and are very happy. In the third situation, a boss criticizes his coworker who has made a costly mistake and "lets him have it".

With great pleasure, the Chinese acted out the stories that we had developed. In the first skit, when two Chinese strangers met, it was apparent that little exchange transpired between the two. There was neither a greeting nor the usual polite sayings, such as, "Could you please tell me what time it is?" or "Thank you, good-bye", as in Europe or America. The whole interaction lacked a greeting, a thankful appreciation, or an acknowledging farewell.

In the second skit, it became apparent that good friends who haven't seen each other in a long time do not shake hands. Their posture was stiff, their eyes shone, and their voices were deeper and softer than usual so that a warmhearted, open feeling was created. But physical contact, such as shaking hands, had not occurred.

In the third skit, the boss reprimanded the coworker for his mistake. His physical stature was unbelievable. With shocking precision, the right index finger of the "boss" repeatedly jutted out and jabbed toward the other person's stomach. The accused employee winced each time, as if he was being stabbed.

Play your vision and fulfill it. Both international companies, Veyhl and Siemens, used the Galli Business Theater to communicate the new business goals to its sales managers.

PHOTOGRAPH BY VEYHL

The participants who observed were overwhelmed by the severity with which someone was being reprimanded. Both the Chinese players had become quite carried away with the skit because they had delved deeply into the emotional situation.

The participants who observed were overwhelmed by the severity with which someone was being reprimanded.

In order to balance out the tension in the room, I asked two German managers to get up and act out the same situation. This would allow the Chinese people to see what body language a German boss would use toward an employee who had made an error when performing a task.

During the reenactment that followed, the German's index finger was also used but not in the direction of the employee. Instead it was raised threateningly toward the ceiling. It was an enlightening experience for the Chinese to see such a difficult emotional situation acted out, just as it had been illuminating for the German and American managers to see how the Chinese treat each other. It was clear, after this heavy, emotionally draining skit that all the participants were exhausted.

In addition, they expressed that they were deeply impressed and could now see with clarity how precise body language can betray emotions.

◎ *Personal habits*

At my suggestion, we all sat in a circle and used the last 15 minutes of our session to relate unusual incidents that the Germans and Americans had experienced with the Chinese and the Chinese with the Americans and the Germans. Once again, the Germans and Americans expressed their disgust at Chinese peoples' habit of spitting loudly in the middle of the street.

And, of course, the Chinese defended their custom by asserting how they could not understand how people could blow their noses as loud as a trumpet in closed rooms and then, indiscreetly, stick the tissue back in their pockets.

The American managers found it strange that, during business meetings, cigarettes were placed in one person's mouth, only to be passed on to others or simply thrown across the room. Then a Chinese manager ironically remarked that during meals everyone eats from each plate so that the "spit is well distributed", which caused astonishment among the Americans. The Chinese people shrugged their shoulders and said, "In China, there is a strong need to bond with friends."

The desire to be able to speak their minds honestly in a friendly atmosphere could clearly be felt.

The desire to be able to speak their minds honestly in a friendly atmosphere could clearly be felt and I spontaneously suggested to the leader of the Training Center that he create a discussion session once a week. At the sessions, differences between the Chinese, the European, and the American cultures could be observed and discussed. All enthusiastically embraced this suggestion.

Exercises

1. *Somebody "invaded my space".*

Describe in detail how someone from a foreign culture invaded your space. What body language did you consciously or unconsciously activate to keep the other person at a distance?

2. *Which greeting rituals of foreign cultures do I know?*

Describe which greeting rituals you have learned in foreign cultures. What effect do they have on you?

3. *Am I prepared to accept the expressions of a foreign culture?*

Openly and honestly describe how you deal with insecurity when your partner uses foreign expressions with you. Do you want to correct him or her? Do you want to understand? Do you have the strength to ask why he or she does it?

4. To what extent do I promote intercultural work?

Describe whether you are careful to arrange in-depth exchanges between people from different cultures in work or private life.

5. I have solved misunderstandings caused by differing cultures.

Describe, using several examples, when you have solved misunderstandings that were caused by the diverse points of view of different cultures. Please consider that this not only concerns foreign cultures but also different social cultures within a country or a business.

Johannes Galli

Johannes Galli was born near Frankfurt, Germany in 1952. He studied literature, philosophy, and history at the University of Freiburg in Breisgau. He pursued his artistic career as an actor and quickly progressed in European theater and on the cultural scene. In the 1980s, he was known throughout Europe as "Clown Galli".

Early in his training he realized, "In acting, the genuine person appears." This became the core of his philosophy that is evidenced by the Galli Method® (the body language awareness training), which uses the lightheartedness and liveliness of spontaneous role-playing as the basis for personal growth and resolution of conflicts in the work environment.

During the course of his international career as a clown, actor, director, musician and author, he has been able to test and constantly develop his communication methods in countless training courses. Several business and research trips to North America and China have allowed him to present his technique with an international element and to create a new source of business training, *Intercultural Training Courses for Communication and Body Language.*

As the founder of the Galli Business Theater, which creates theater pieces for companies, and as the author and director of motivational theater, Johannes Galli has worked for prominent business enterprises worldwide. Since 1989, the demand has continued to grow for Galli Business Theater presentations that are designed to strengthen intercultural bonds and mutual understanding.

The Galli Publishing House— Teaching and Learning Materials

Additional information about the Galli Method® can be found in the many books Johannes Galli has authored. They can be used as an interesting and informational resource for personal communication training, as well as, business communication training.

Additional books by Johannes Galli

The Clown as a Healer

Body Language and Communication

Dynamic Story Telling

Communication Theater

The Seven Kellerkinder®

Dance Meditations–Movement, Butterfly, Dance Meditation

Dance Meditations–Animals, Evolutionary Myth

Dance Meditations–The Seven Kellerkinder®, Clown

If you are interested in more information about the Galli Method® in the field of Galli Business Theater, Galli Training, and a list of products of the Galli Publishing House visit our web site:

http://www.galli-group.com

For any questions, you are welcome to contact us directly via e-mail. We will be happy to respond:

e-mail: publishing@galli-group.com

Intercultural Communication and Body Language

Novartis Pharmaceuticals used the Galli Business Theater and its clowns to train coaching skills. Everybody was curious to see if the clown would succeed in changing a pessimist into an optimist . . .
he did.

PHOTOGRAPH BY JAN GALLI